BEING SELF-DISCIPLINED

LEARN AND TRAIN YOUR MENTAL
STRENGTH TO OBTAIN SELF-DISCIPLINE

George M. Davis

Table of Contents

Introduction

Self-discipline is, without a doubt, one of the essential life skills everyone, and I mean *everyone*, should have. There are, of course, plenty of other important life skills everyone should master, such as people skills, time and money management skills, survival skills, professional skills, communication skills, and more.

Reread the last sentence. Do you know what all these other skills have in common?

If you answered self-discipline, you're correct! It would help if you had the discipline to master many different life skills effectively. Skills that are important for your success at work, at school, at home, or anywhere else for that matter.

Now, achieving self-discipline is *not easy*. Don't trust anyone who tells you that. To achieve self-discipline, you need to have the ability to *control* your emotions, your body, and your mind.

It's the ability to rise beyond your weaknesses and be strong enough to resist temptations that may come your way (*and you will have plenty of those, trust me*). If you think doing that is easy, then you're probably superhuman or maybe even a robot!

We may not share the same weaknesses, but as humans, we **all** have flaws. It could be something material or immaterial, and it could be tangible or non-tangible; it can even be a living thing like other human beings or animals. Every time you see these objects, these weaknesses, your resolve weakens, and you lose your self-control. In some cases, maybe even your self-respect.

Overcoming your weaknesses is necessary for you to be successful at disciplining yourself. Why? You simply don't have a choice.

Temptations and obstacles will litter your path to success, and you must avoid these at all costs! If you fail, you will also fail big time on self-discipline if you give in to your weaknesses.

If you've always wanted to achieve or excel at something, such as sports, academics, arts, music, and more, you need to have the self-discipline to go after what you want and chase after your dreams. You don't just sit around and wait for something to happen. Because nothing will happen, you have to put in the 5 work, most probably over a long period, so you can achieve whatever it is you're aiming for.

By the time you finish reading the last chapter in this book, you'll know everything there is to know about self-discipline and how you can use it to build your mental strength to resist temptation so you can finally reach your goals.

Chapter 1:

Identify Your 'Why'?

It's effortless to say you're going to accomplish something, *anything*, in the next 12 months. You can say you're going to be 20 pounds lighter, or you'll be living in Europe after a year, or you can even say you're going to find the love of your life soon and tie the knot in the next 12 months!

You can do many things, be in many places, and meet loads of new people in under a year. You have an *infinite* number of possible goals you can choose to achieve.

Your chosen goal could be in response to a dare from your friends or maybe a personal challenge you want to take on. No matter the reason behind your sudden desire to succeed at something new, *you need one essential skill* to achieve that goal.

Can you guess what that skill is? It's self-discipline, of course.

Committing to a long-term goal is the *beginning* of your self-discipline journey. Once you've done a mental handshake with yourself or signed on an imaginary dotted line confirming your commitment to a specific goal, then your self-discipline should kick into high gear.

You need to lock yourself in and buckle up, so you don't get left behind in the marathon to reach your goal. You need the stamina and the strength to surpass and overcome all obstacles to meet your goal.

Choose A Feasible Goal

Before you can begin, you need to know the answer to the question, "What is your why?"

What do you hope to achieve with your goal? What's your end game?

If you don't know the answer to this question, you need to rethink your goal seriously.

Is it even feasible? Is it something you can hope to do within the timeframe you've specified? If you've assessed your goal correctly and you've done the mental gymnastics to confirm 8 it is indeed feasible for you, then congratulations. You've done a great job with the first step!

If you think you made a mistake setting the goal and you **don't** think it's feasible at all, you're welcome to back out or cross it out of your list and replace it with a more realistic goal.

There's no need to push yourself into doing something highly improbable or even impossible for you to achieve.

Some people may say nothing is impossible. But I beg to disagree.

We are not created equal. We all know for a fact that some people have more financial resources than others. Some are just naturally athletic. Some will always be better looking than the people around them. Others are still really blessed not to have to work hard for something other people need to work their backsides off for! They are the lucky ones, the exceptions to the rule. They've been given a natural head start whether they like it or not (*though I'm pretty sure they want it just fine!*).

Specify Your Goal

Now that you know your goal is realistic and can be done within your specified timeframe, you need to ask yourself if your goal is specific enough. Some plans are just too general, like wanting to be rich or thin in 6 months. These are just generic goals. Anyone can work towards these goals, but what does it mean for you?

To make sure your goal sticks in your mind, you need to make your goal as specific as possible to make it appear natural.

Don't just say you want to lose weight. For **women**, you can say something along these lines (if you're a guy, skip to the following example below):

"I'll do whatever it takes to lose 10 pounds by December, so I can wear that hot, red dress I saw

today at the shopping mall. My belly won't sag, and I'll look perfect in that dress. I'll have my hair made up in a beehive because that's the kind of hairdo that would look great with that dress. Oh, and I'll wear my black stiletto too, and my feet won't hurt as it does now because I'd lose all the excess weight!"

When you read that paragraph, it painted a pretty picture on your mind, didn't it? And you can see yourself wearing that red dress!

For the **guys** reading this book, your specific goal can be something like this:

"I'll lose the flab around my belly in 8 months. I'll exercise every day. I'll lift weights, do plenty of cardio, and box with somebody in the gym. In 8 months, my girlfriend/wife will be proud of me, I'll be proud of myself, and we can go to the

beach, and people will marvel at my well-sculpted body".

The examples I've given above sound so much better than just saying the generic, "I want to lose weight." A generic goal is not 10 going to drive you to change your habits, but a particular purpose will be.

Visualize Your Goal

At this point, you now know your goal is feasible *and* specific enough. To make it come to life, you need to visualize your goal.

Yes, in the previous section, you saw the goal come to life in your mind's eye, but you need to make the vision tangible in this section.

You need to put your goal on paper. You need to transfer the vision you saw in your mind to paper. You can look for high-quality photos of your plan. Say, for example, if your goal is to move into your dream house with a red roof and a blue fence within 5 years, you can look for images online of homes with similar characteristics.

If you can't find a suitable image online, consider having it drawn or painted professionally. Ask the artist to make your vision as accurate as possible. When we say realistic, make it so that you can imagine feeling and even smelling your dream house just by looking at its drawing or painting.

Then, to never lose sight of your goal, make sure you put the printout/drawing/painting in an area of your houses which you frequent, such as your bedroom or your home office. Maybe even the kitchen. Anywhere you can see your 'dream house' so you're constantly reminded of what you're aiming to achieve shortly.

Visualize The Process

In the previous section, I've shown you how to visualize your goal to make it seem tangible and within arms' reach. This section will show you another powerful technique you can use to make your goal even more achievable and more realistic.

This technique is similar to the previous one; however, instead of visualizing the goal, you'll be *imagining the process of achieving your goal.*

In our previous example, our goal was to buy our dream house in 5 years. Using this method, what you need to do first is you need to plan out the process or the steps you need to take so you can buy your dream house.

You can say that to achieve this goal, you'd need to work hard to *get a promotion at work and get a raise*, then you'll be able to *save more money* to *afford a down payment* on the house.

You can then print out images of an *ecstatic person finally getting promoted at work* and a picture *of a truckload of money* to represent the amount you'll need to save to buy your house.

This process-oriented visualization technique is compelling because it helps prepare your mind for the challenges you'll be facing.

Yes, you want the house, but you know (and you're ready) to do a great job at work and save up some serious cash so you can pay for your new house!

As you've learned in this chapter, knowing and visualizing your

"why" takes a lot of self-discipline as the entire process is extraordinarily detail-oriented. It takes a special kind of discipline to unearth and uncover the specifics of your "why," which will ultimately be the foundation for realizing your long-term goals.

Chapter 2:

Be Accountable to Others and Self-Accountability

This chapter will learn why you *must not* stop visualizing your goal, as I showed in the first chapter. Instead, you need to take the next step: to be accountable to yourself and another person (your accountability buddy).

Let's start with self-accountability and why this is important in building your self-discipline.

Self-Accountability

If you practice self-accountability, you have a deep sense of ethics.

You don't lie to yourself, and you don't deliberately take shortcuts that could eventually backfire. In short, you are honest with yourself, and you take responsibility for your actions. This is very important when building self-discipline because it keeps you in line, it keeps you in check, and it keeps you contained, so you don't beyond the narrow path you've set for yourself on the way to fulfilling your goal.

Being self-accountable means, you have integrity. If you do something detrimental to your goal, you acknowledge it.

You don't hide it, and you don't attempt to write it off. Instead, you face it, and you promise yourself you won't do it again. And you continue on your path to fulfilling your goal, all the while keeping your actions in line with your plan.

21

So how do you keep yourself accountable?

Most experts suggest keeping a journal to write your thoughts and daily experiences in. You can use an old-fashioned made-of-paper journal, and you can sign up for online journal services if you're tech-savvy or use a word processor like Microsoft Word.

For the younger generation, a mobile app might be more your thing as kids these days are bound to be glued to their iPhones and their Android smartphones.

Whatever you choose to write on, make sure you put it to good use. That means WRITE on it.

What do you write down?

Write down everything you do from the time you wake up to just before you go to sleep. All your experiences for the day, your adventures, anything that's a mini-step to reaching your goal. Write down your tasks and accomplishments at work, any new stuff you've learned, what you did well and what you could improve on.

Additionally, you could also write down your negative thoughts and any doubts or fears you may have about your goal. You could then write down your responses to your worries. Doing this is somewhat cathartic and the next time you feel down again, look up your positive answers, and it should hopefully bring you out of your funk.

Journals help keep track of where your money and your time are going. Are you spending enough time working on achieving your goal, or are you wasting it on watching TV or lying in bed doing nothing?

Remember, you're accountable to yourself. So if you're procrastinating, you're not doing something good. You need to stop such behavior and focus on doing positive actions that will help you reach your goal.

Do this journal exercise for a month or so until it becomes ingrained in your mind, and it becomes a habit – a very positive habit that will heighten your sense of accountability.

Accountability To Others

Making yourself accountable to yourself and others is the perfect combination for success. It's like having someone watch over you internally (self-accountability) and externally (accountability to others).

When you make yourself accountable to others, especially someone you look up to, it challenges you to make sure you don't fail and disappoint them. You're seeking their stamp of approval and admiration, and you're going to do everything it takes to get that.

When choosing another person to be your accountability buddy, select someone you trust. Someone you like and admire. Maybe someone with the same personality as yours so compatibility won't be an issue, and you can be comfortable with that person.

It can be your spouse, partner, parent, best friend, or even a professional mentor or coach. Whoever you choose, remember you're leaving yourself wide open; you're leaving yourself highly vulnerable, so choose someone you can trust with your life and who you know will not betray you. You are seeking their help after all, and if you choose the wrong kind of person instead of helping you, they can jeopardize your goals.

You don't want that to happen.

What's great about being accountable to someone is that they will tell you straight up and give you some good kicking in your pants if you fall off the wagon. They'll encourage you, and 17 motivate you to continue pursuing your dreams, your goals, and they'll remind you constantly to do what you're supposed to do.

Now that you know about accountability and its role in developing your self-discipline, you need to find that unique buddy and start working on your journal.

Chapter 3:
Moving Towards Good
Self-Discipline Through
Good Habits

Developing good habits takes time, but since these are the main foundations for mastering self-discipline, I can assure you that time is well spent.

Habits are actions or behavior patterns that you do out of rote, out of repetition. It's become so ingrained in your daily life, and you've become so used to it that you start doing it involuntarily.

You don't even need to think about making your habit before you do it; you do.

Good v/s Bad Habits

There are two types of habits. Good habits and bad habits. If you want to master self-discipline, you have to let go of your bad habits and replace them with new, positive ones.

Bad habits are negative behavior patterns that are a hindrance or a roadblock to your mental and physical health, including any goals you've set for yourself. Laziness, unhealthy eating habits, rude behavior, bullying, swearing, and procrastination are examples of bad habits that do nothing for you and do not contribute to your growth.

Of course, saying goodbye to a bad habit is easier said than done and is practically impossible to do overnight. It's called a habit because you do it involuntarily, so it's going to take a lot of self-conscious effort on your part to stop making your bad habits.

Some experts say it will take a minimum of 3 weeks to a month for a person to forego his bad habits. It will take plenty of mental and physical effort to do this, but you'll be better off without your bad habits weighing you down in the end.

So how do you replace a bad habit with good practice?

Good habits come in many different forms. There are *simple habits* and physically demanding patterns that might be challenging to master at first.

Assuming you're also working on breaking your bad habits, it would be best to start with a simple and easy-to-implement pattern. After all, you don't want to overwhelm yourself and get stressed with the thought of doing too much at once. When crushed, some people tend to procrastinate, so working on too many habits at once may backfire on you.

To narrow down some good habits you should pick up on, write down a list of patterns you would like to acquire. If you want to pick up an exciting but complicated habit, you can break it down into more minor bite-sized ways. Remember, it's easier to implement simple practices than highly complicated ones. Once you've written your proposed habits, write a score beside each pattern and choose the one that came out easiest based on your scoring system.

Work on this habit every day for at least a month. Remember how in Chapter 2 we talked about journals and how you should be writing down everything you do in a day? Well, make sure this habit-forming activity of yours gets written down too. And don't forget to review your journal every week or so just to see how you're getting along with your progress.

When your new habit has finally become a *natural habit*, it's time to work on the following positive pattern you should acquire. Just rinse and repeat this process and try to retain as many positive habits as you can – practices that will help you fulfill your tasks at home, at work, or anywhere else.

Here's why **building one good habit** at a time is essential for self-discipline success:

1. You're taking action. Even just the act of trying to get a new habit will require self-discipline. The more you take action, the more your new pattern gets ingrained.

2. Your chances of failure are significantly reduced. Your good habits will be ingrained in

your brain that you do it by rote, without conscious thinking. If you committed the proper action to memory, failing would be minimized.

3. It helps you build confidence and momentum. You're training yourself to be confident with one good habit. If you succeed, you'll feel pretty sure, and you'd be encouraged to take on another positive pattern.

4. It requires you to be responsible and accountable. Forming an excellent new habit will help you to become accountable since you've tasked yourself to do it repeatedly.

Here are a few examples of good habits:

1. Get up early in the morning (don't stay in bed until noon).

2. Exercise daily (even if you're busy, find a way to fit it into your schedule).

3. Eat a full breakfast (this is the first meal of the day, so don't skip it).

4. Drink plenty of water every day (stop drinking too many soft drinks).

The Morning Ritual Habit

Many experts claim the morning ritual habit is one of the essential habits everyone should practice. Research has shown that a shocking 90% of successful individuals have a morning ritual habit. CEOs of big companies such as Twitter CEO Jack Dorsey, PepsiCo CEO Indra Nooyi, and high-powered politicians like Margaret Thatcher wake up early in the morning to do their rituals before heading off to work.

Waking up early in the morning when everything's quiet is great for meditating, praying, or reading inspiring books and quotes.

During this particular time, turn off your gadgets and focus on renewing your mind. This is your time, so feel free to update your journal, write down your thoughts, and plan your entire day. Doing this helps you get your mind and body ready for the day ahead. You can even identify your two most important tasks for the day and try to get them done first thing in the morning so that you're free to do less important tasks by the afternoon.

Another essential activity you can squeeze in during your morning ritual is exercising. It clears your head, and running on a treadmill for even just 5-10 minutes will reduce stress and help boost your metabolism.

Lastly, another successful habit people do in their morning rituals is preparing their food for the whole day, right up to dinner. Sure, you can eat out from time to time, but it's so much better and healthier to prepare your food at home, especially if you're counting calories. Eating out is like a calorie-fest where you get twice, thrice, or even 5 times the average calories you get from cooking your food!

For night owls, adapting to this lifestyle and changing habits would probably be tremendously tricky at first. Try adapting slowly. Sleep 15 minutes earlier each night to wake up 15 minutes earlier as well.

Do this cycle until you get used to sleeping in early and waking up early too.

Implementing the morning ritual habit is very highly recommended by time management and behavior experts. Yes, it won't be easy, but this is why you work on developing *one practice at a time*. Do this process slowly over weeks. You should see some progress in a month or so, and you'd then be more productive, and you'll have a more straightforward path to reaching your goals.

Developing positive habits is very important for your success. Chapter 5 discusses more healthy habits you can pick up on, so scroll down to that chapter for more ideas!

Chapter 4:
Eliminating Obstacles to Disciplining Yourself

Self-discipline is a very personal endeavor. You can indeed get help and support from other people such as your spouse, family, and friends, but to succeed, YOU must believe that YOU can discipline YOURSELF. If you ask *other* people to punish you, then that no longer falls under the realm of **self**-discipline.

You might think you know yourself, and you're 100% confident that you can impose self-discipline to achieve some goal you've set for yourself. You'd be enthusiastic and very optimistic at first, but later on, you'll notice your interest in chasing your dream is waning

Quite possibly, you may even have already decided you're throwing in the towel and just giving up altogether.

If you read chapter 1, you should already know your "why" for disciplining yourself. You should know for sure by now that your goal is feasible and not something impossible for you to do. So if you did all that and you're plan is indeed possible, but you're still giving up, then you're looking at *obstacles* that are blocking your path to success.

There are many different kinds of obstacles that may come your way. Some blocks will be external and permanent, and you have zero control over it, at which point you'd have to accept your fate and move on.

But if the obstacle is temporary and you know for a fact that it's not going to be there permanently, then you need to work on removing it from your path so you can continue pursuing your goal.

The Common Obstacles You Must Fight Against

The biggest obstacle to your goals and your dreams are all in your head. That's right; **mental obstacles** are your biggest enemy. We have millions of thoughts and ideas swirling in our brains all the time, and not all of them are going to be positive.

Many would-bes are downright harmful. Here are some perfect examples of negative thoughts that can obstruct your road to success:

- I can't do it. It's too darn complicated.

- I'm too busy right now. I'll do it later.

- I'm going to fail miserably.

- What will people think of me if I fail?

- What's going to happen if I succeed? My life would change.

- They're all the better than me. I'm never going to beat them.

- They don't like me. They're looking at me like I'm going to fail already.

- I quit.

Sound familiar? I'm sure you've had one or all of these negative thoughts running through your head at one time or another. Maybe even now.

So how do you overcome these mental obstacles?

I'm not even going to say it's easy because curing something mentally is different from curing a physical ailment. But a good start is by standing tall and believing in yourself. *Self-confidence is key to obliterating mental roadblocks*.

Be firm in your decision and stop doubting yourself. The key takeaway here is if you don't believe in yourself, no one will. That's a fact.

The second obstacle you would have to overcome would be **physical obstacles**. If an accident occurs and you're left with a bodily injury during chasing down your dreams, then this is an obstacle. But don't despair because plenty of people, including superstar athletes, have fallen and gotten injured, but many are still able to rise back up and continue their journey.

Look at Stephen Hawking. He's disabled physically, but he has a brilliant, gifted mind, and he never let his disability hamper him down. Instead, he looked for innovative and ingenious solutions to enable himself to live relatively everyday life.

The third obstacle lying in your path would be **financial obstacles**. If your goal involves funding from outside sources or investors, then you need to work hard to get them to trust you and your business model, so they'll invest and spend their money on you. If you don't get a yes from a single investor, don't despair.

There are other ways to drum up the cash. If you're determined, passionate, and driven to succeed, sooner or later, investors are going to come knocking at your door.

The fourth obstacle would be **time**. Having too much or too little time can both present themselves as obstacles to your success. If you have *too much time*, you can easily get distracted. If you don't have the self-discipline, you could get bored and do stuff you wouldn't normally do if you were busy. So try to be active and be productive. It's okay to relax from time to time but not too much.

As the saying goes, *"Idle hands are the devil's workshop."*

A second scenario would be a *lack of time*. If you have too little time to chase your dreams, then you need to FIND the time. You need to make some room for your goals. No matter how busy you get, it would help if you found pockets of time to devote to working on your dream.

In Chapter 3, I recommended you pick up the morning rituals habit so you can squeeze in some personal time before your day begins. This is the perfect time to work on your goals and your dreams.

The fifth obstacle on our list would be **distractions or temptations**. If you don't have self-discipline, you'll be fair game for getting distracted easily.

Are your friends inviting you to a party? Party versus boring dream? It's a no-brainer, right? Party, here I come!

Instead of working on your goals, you're going to go to the party.

This would, of course, be the wrong decision. If you're the partying type, you'd need to work doubly hard on your self-discipline so you can resist this particular weakness. If you're able to

45

conquer this, your path to success just got a whole lot clearer.

There are plenty more obstacles that could come your way. We can't list them all here as everyone has different goals and different dreams. Each plan will have its own set of obstacles you need to overcome to succeed.

Chapter 5:How to Take Care of Your Body to Build Self-Discipline

Eating a balanced diet, exercising regularly, getting enough sleep, and minimizing stressors in your environment all contribute to your good health. We only have one body. If we want to survive well into our old age, we have to learn how to take care of it. In this chapter, I'll share some handy health tips which you can use to ensure your body is in tiptop shape. Remember to consult with your doctor first before attempting to do any of the information I'll discuss below.

Eat Healthily

Reinforcing positive and healthy eating habits helps ensure you get enough nutrition for your body. I'm not talking about eating fast food here. I'm talking about healthy, home-cooked meals that are chock full of vitamins and minerals for you.

Here are some good eating habits you should develop:

- Eat vegetables at every meal

- Eat whole foods as these are rich in phytochemicals

- Eat protein every day to ward off muscle loss

- Drink plenty of water (at least 8 glasses a day)

- Supplement your meals with a multivitamin and maybe fish oil as well

- Eat slowly for better digestion and greater satisfaction with your meal

- Use a smaller plate to help make you feel full faster

- Don't go back for seconds and thirds

Exercise Regularly

Exercise has plenty of benefits for our bodies. Aside from the obvious physical benefits, exercise produces the brain's chemical endorphin, which acts as a natural painkiller and helps reduce stress.

Exercising regularly takes a lot of self-discipline to muster, and as such, you become more conscious of what goes inside your body.

You tend to drink less alcohol, smoke fewer cigarettes, and you're more motivated to eat healthy food. You'll soon find yourself replacing your bad habits (such as smoking and drinking) with good productive ones such as better study habits, improved spending habits, and more.

In Chapter 3, we discussed the morning rituals habit which many successful individuals have adopted. One of the rituals you could do during your private 'me time' is exercise.

Morning is the best time to exercise right before you have breakfast and drive off to work as you are in a fasted state, increasing the fat-burning effect. To burn even more calories, you should also consider going for a quick run.

Get A Good Night's Sleep

Getting at least 6 hours of sleep at night is very important to help improve your self-discipline. Sleep deprivation raises stress hormone levels, and you'll soon find yourself losing not just self-control, but you'll also be easily distracted, and you'll suffer from short-term memory loss too.

Here are some good sleeping habits to develop:

- Avoid drinking coffee and other drinks with caffeine as this is a stimulant (will keep you awake).

- Remove all electronics from your bedroom. If you've got a TV inside, it's time to move it somewhere else. Please leave your mobile phone outside as well, or at least keep it silent and out of arm's reach.

- Use your bedroom for two activities only: sleeping and sex.

- Don't exercise before bedtime. Do it early in the day as it helps promote restful sleep at night.

- If you ate a large meal, don't go straight to bed. Wait about an hour before you lie down, so you don't get indigestion.

- Avoid eating sugary snacks at night as sugar is also a stimulant.

Avoid Getting Stressed Out

Ideally, we want to live stress-free lives, but as well all know this isn't possible. With an endless supply of stressors, no one can escape stress. We can, however, manage and minimize it.

Stress can weaken your self-discipline. When you're stressed, you tend not to think; clearly, you may think irrationally, and you may end up making the wrong decisions.

Here are some good habits that will help reduce your stress:

- Do some breathing exercises to help control anxiety. A good practice would be the Navy Seals breathing technique which goes like this:

o Inhale deeply (4 counts)

o Exhale (4 counts)

o Repeat the cycle for 4 minutes o

Do this several times a day

- Listen to some classical or instrumental music. Many people like to listen to classical music while working or studying as it helps improve focus, and unlike vocal music, you don't get distracted by singing along to lyrics.

- You can try meditating in a quiet room. Let your thoughts flow freely and acknowledge whatever floats to the surface.

Don't fight whatever you see in your mind's eye. Just accept what you see, and you'll soon find your stress melting away.

- Try helping others in need. When you shift your focus from your stressful life to someone who needs your help, you temporarily forget your problems. It also gets you out of the house and gets you in contact with other people.

I've listed down several helpful and practical tips that you can apply in your life today. And discussed in Chapter 2, write down all your experiences in a journal. Whether you ran a few miles this morning or you tried meditating or volunteering, write it down. This process is hugely important to help keep yourself accountable and make sure you are indeed taking good care of your body.

Chapter 6:
Stress and Self-Discipline

As I have mentioned in the previous chapter, managing stress is essential if you want to discipline yourself for the long term. Being unable to cope with stress can lead to health issues which can cause even *more* stress for you and your family, and you certainly don't want that to happen.

No one can avoid stress – it's a part of life. Even the wealthiest among us suffer from anxiety. And the same is true for those in the lower end of the financial spectrum.

Not all stress is bad. There exists a good kind of stress.

Perhaps you've already experienced it, but you didn't recognize it as being good stress.

Good Stress vs. Bad Stress

Good stress, also known as *eustress*, is beneficial short-term stress which encourages or motivates you to accomplish more. Yes, you might have sweaty palms and a racing heart, but if it's in response to a challenge *you think you can overcome*, then it's good stress. .

When you're running a marathon, you'd feel stressed about the challenge. But at the same time, you're getting a whole lot of benefits such as physical exercise, that incredible feeling of accomplishment when you finish the race, *and if you have a shot at winning*, the euphoria of coming in first and beating everybody else!

If you were running a marathon and you have no hope of ever crossing the finish line due to some physical injury or a mental breakdown, then that's the **wrong kind of stress**. It's terrible because *you have little to no control over the situation,* and you feel helpless. You tend to have pessimistic thoughts in the face of bad stress.

Good stress can give you a rush of adrenaline which engages your fight or flight response. It can propel you forward and motivate you to put your best foot forward. Some people like waiting until the last minute to do things because that's when eustress and adrenaline kick in, and it gives them the motivation to focus on finishing their tasks! If you are one of them, the good news is that this kind of stress won't do any harm to your body because it's just short-term stress.

However, suppose you keep on delaying tasks and projects until the last minute because you're waiting for the all-powerful eustress to motivate you. In that case, there's a good chance you could end up becoming overwhelmed, and you'd lose control of the situation.

Regularly overwhelming your body with *too much work* in *too little time* will stress you out. This is the type of stress that can kill you. This is the kind of stress that requires lengthy recuperation through extended rest or maybe even a trip to the hospital.

If you find yourself in such a dire situation, you need to work on your self-discipline to don't go off the deep end. You have to regain control and not allow yourself to wait until the last minute to get some work, tasks, or chores done.

The Role Of Self-Discipline In Managing Stress

With self-discipline, you can minimize or even avoid getting into overly stressful situations. If you're disciplined, you're not going to look for the *high* that eustress gives you. This means that if you find yourself being more productive and efficient in challenging situations, then you're not going to seek that *rush* every single time because it could come back and bite you in your behind!

If you're faced with several looming deadlines, and you know you can't possibly meet all of them, your body will think it's under threat and will slowly start shutting down to preserve itself. This is the ' *freeze'* reaction from your body's **fight-flight-freeze response,** which occurs whenever we face challenging situations.

Haven't you noticed that you usually freeze up whenever you think there's no more hope and the odds of succeeding are close to nil? This is precisely what happens when our bodies go through too much bad stress.

In the case of eustress, or when you believe there's a good chance you'll succeed with the challenge in front of you, your body takes on the *fight or flight* response. This usually kicks in when there's even the slightest hope of survival. You are willing to face the challenge head-on (fight) or run away as fast as you can (flight) to survive. This 'fight or flight response will give you the extra burst of energy you need to defeat, outrun, and outdistance your problem situation.

Having self-discipline comes in very handy when you are left with two choices – avoid stress or face stress head-on. If you are disciplined, you'll do all you can to prevent stress, even good stress, because you know that it can quickly turn into bad stress. You'll do your best to complete your tasks early on in the day; you're not going to wait until the very last minute because you feel more effective when cramming on functions!

Your self-discipline will help you manage your time wisely, and it will save you from hours of unnecessary frustration. Being disciplined means you'll face your challenges head-on, and you'll diligently lay out a plan to conquer them to succeed.

Highly disciplined individuals are excellent planners – they map out both their short-term and long-term goals – and they'll see to it that they'll stick to their plans while resisting temptation mightily. This is how disciplined people manage stress and succeed in doing so.

On the other hand, if you don't have discipline, then you'll cave in to temptations easily. If your deadlines are quite some time away, you won't be thinking about how you can finish your task well ahead of the deadline.

Instead, you'll fool around (self-gratification), and when the deadline is near, that's when you'll start working (cramming). Of course, this leaves you with, more often than not, little to no room for mistakes, so when things go awry (as they often will), then you'll land in hot water. So, start being responsible today and start working on your self-discipline.

How to Reduce Stress to Live Longer and Happier

Reducing stress can help you live longer, healthier, and happier. When you move to live longer and healthier, happiness often follows pursuit. Stress is pressure, or physiological responses, which when pressure occurs, the body and mind will respond. Most times, the person feels threatened, or fears change or else feels challenged when stress occurs. Nowadays, we have to work twice as hard to survive, which has increased the rates of illnesses stemming from stress.

The number of people today suffering has reached far past 1 million each year. Stress is a positive influence, however. When you feel stress, you want to turn the negative energy into positive thinking. How does it work?

First, remember to tell yourself well each day, for no one knows what tomorrow will bring. Furthermore, learn to live one day at a time, unless you are overwhelmed with stress, and then learn to live one second at a time. If you are using alcohol or drugs to relieve constant tension, you want to consider other healthier tactics. If you are losing sleep and find that alcohol helps you sleep, remember that you lose REM sleep when you drink. REM is the dream state, which is essential.

You can go to the local pharmacist and purchase Melatonin supplements, which will relax the nerves and help you sleep. Melatonin costs a few bucks and will save you more than spending on alcohol or drugs to loosen. If you are unfamiliar with signs of stress, emotional symptoms, mental symptoms, physical symptoms, or behaviors that stem from stress, we can consider a few details now.

The Signs:

Irritability is a sign that a person is over-stressed. When you feel edgy, uptight, or feel impatient is taking control, you are likely overwhelmed with stress. Sensitivity, pessimistic thinking, and taking offense to what others say to you are signs of stress. If you are twitching nervously, biting your nails, pulling hair, or jiggling the knees, you likely are experiencing stress. Nausea, constipation, diarrhea, excessive smoking is all signs of stress.

Mental Symptoms

When you often forget or find it hard to concentrate, likely the mind is overwhelmed with thoughts. Likewise, when you find it hard to make decisions (Small or Large) and find yourself obsessing, you are likely overwhelmed with stress. Fatigue and overwhelming feelings of pressure is a sign of stress.

Emotional Symptoms:

Emotional symptoms stemming from stress may include low self-esteem, anxiety, panic attacks, anger, resentment, ready to cry often, moodiness, nightmares, and inability to laugh.

Physiology or Physical Symptoms:

When you feel stressed, you may experience tension in the muscles and fatigue. You will likely experience back, head, shoulder, and neck aches.

Your eyes may feel tired, and the muscles may twitch, especially around the corners of your eyes. Often the jaw feels stiff, while the mouth feels dry.

Often the palms of the hands will feel sweaty, while the fingers will feel cold. You may experience heartburn and indigestion often, as well as bladder and urinary problems. You may also experience palpitations of the heart, weight gain and loss, headaches, colds, hyperventilation, and so forth when you are overwhelmed with stress.

Behavioral Signs:

Often when a person is overwhelmed with stress, the person will feel angry and explode when miscommunications occur. The person may feel aggressive and talk persistently, as well as often interrupting others who speak. Sometimes the person will withdraw from society or social gatherings. The person may stop taking care of him or herself and could show signs of obsessive-compulsive behaviors.

As you can see, stress is a hazard to health, happiness, and life unless you learn to use stress as your friend.

Live Longer and Healthier in How to Relate to Stress

Emotional stress is leading to stress, which can have a positive effect on everyone.

Mental stress, physical stress, and emotional stress are different types of stress that a person can experience. Too much stress can have adverse side effects on the body and mind.

71

Having no stress can also give one an unexciting life. By looking at a typical week, one can identify the problems or situations with a person experiencing anxiousness or stress.

Once a person can find the problem or situation, they will address it and remove it.

Do you spend a half-hour a day worrying? This could be a good experience.

The doctor report spending a half-hour a day worrying can help to become less anxious. Are you a worrier? You will not have to worry anymore, as persistent worriers do not experience more severe troubles than other people do. We think we have more severe problems and try to handle the issues by not thinking about them.

Exercise, exercise, and do more exercising. Why? When a person looks and feels great, they will feel less stress, assume more self-assurance; exercise will help give life-long expectance with the aging process by slowing down the process. Exercising every day will help keep a healthier life and help reduce stress.

Arthritis will set in if you don't use muscles and joints. This can harm the body and its long life span. Joints will tighten up, muscles will weaken, and the outward appearance will show with age as a person gets older. Exercising a person can keep the joints stretchy, avoiding fragile bones as age bone can break with falling. As most of us know, with aging, hips are usually broken very quickly, with the slightest fall.

Relaxing is known to help reduce stress, which you can learn to relax by reading a good book. Reading will help take your mind of daily stressors.

Getting the body to relax, stretching out the muscles, limps joints to do nothing. Listening to music, maybe just water falling, a storm, or favorite CD you have. Close your eyes and relax. Or perhaps just a good crossword puzzle or a hobby you can help take the stress from the day. One thing with relaxing it will help you when life challenges come your way.

Are you having trouble sleeping? Are you getting enough sleep? Sleeping is essential to reduce stress in your daily life. Mattresses could play a part in sleep loss, thus getting a new bed could help you achieve proper rest.

You may even change your bedroom, including sheets, blanket, and so forth.

Making good sleeping habits a routine is a way to reduce stress and to live a longer and healthier life.

Eating healthy: Eating healthy foods will benefit a person in every way possible in their life. Eating maintains the body with proper vitamins, iron, fats, and carbohydrates to have a healthy functioning body. Without appropriate foods and nutrients, a body can become sluggish; organs can be harmed without proper nutrition, and the brain does not function well without feeding it.

Healthy eating the right foods for the body, getting enough and proper sleep, learning and taking time out to relax, and exercising to keep joints free from

arthritis and stiffing. These great functions will help a person with stress live a long, happy life and become healthy, free from high blood pressure, high cholesterol, and other heart-related diseases as a person experience aging.

It is not too late to start with a healthy life to expand your life with aging.

Check with your doctor for more information; research on the internet for more tips and ideas for staying healthy. HGH (Human Growth Hormone) can also help you live longer, healthier, and happier.

Chapter 7:

Set Boundaries and Learn to Say 'No'

Self-discipline allows you to pursue your goals without falling prey to various distractions and temptations that will stop you from achieving your goals. And you can do this by setting boundaries and learning to say "no" when the occasion calls for it.

Saying "yes" might be the polite thing to do, but if it is detrimental to your success, saying "no" is the best course of action for you.

We'd love to say "yes" all the time to people who need us, people who want us to do something for them. Sometimes we might feel like we're being taken advantage of, but we usually shrug these feelings off because we want to please people and hate disappointing them. This is especially true for people who mean a lot to us - like family and friends – and people we look up to, such as mentors and respected community members.

Setting Boundaries For Yourself

Boundaries *protect* you from those who'd take advantage of you and your time. It lets you define your space. It lets other people know what's most important to you and how you want to be treated.

When setting boundaries, you have to know your values and limits, what you like and don't like, and what you're willing to compromise on. You have to stick to your boundaries and be ready to compromise, especially if doing so will help you reach your goals faster.

Having boundaries in place keeps you honest and authentic with yourself. You know when to say "yes" and when to say "no." If you don't have any boundaries, you'll end up saying "yes" all the time.

Now there's nothing wrong with saying "yes" and helping other people, but if you sacrifice too much of yourself and your time, you're left with *nothing* for yourself.

Some people love taking advantage of others they perceive as weak because it makes them feel better about themselves. If you keep on saying "yes," even when you want to say "no," these people are going to continue asking until you finally set boundaries and learn to say "no."

Saying "No" Is A Shortcut To Your Success

Every time you say "yes" to something that's a *deterrent* or *distraction* from your goal, then you're only making your journey to success *much longer*. It's therefore essential to note that if you want to reach your goals or dreams in the shortest amount of time possible, you have to learn to say "no."

If you aren't too private a person and you don't mind sharing your long-term goals with others, you can try mentioning your goals to them *as a disclaimer* right before you say "no" to whatever they are tempting you with.

For instance, if someone is inviting you to go out for a night of partying and drinking, and you know that wasting your time on frivolous activities like that won't exactly help you

81

achieve anything, then just tell your friend something like, "Sorry, no, I'm busy tonight."

If you think telling your friend the valid reason for your rejection will insult or hurt him, say something else and reject them gently (some people can be sensitive to surrender).

Rejection of people is not easy. Sometimes you may even end up debating with someone because they won't accept your sacrifice, and they won't listen to your reasons for saying "no." Most of us probably have a few authoritative friends like that who thinks they're always right and refuse to listen to opposing arguments.

Getting them to accept your rejection might be hard but if it brings you a *step closer to your long-term goals*, then by all means, please say "no." Strengthening your resolve to say "no."

And standing your ground helps improve your self-discipline and self-control. So it's a win-win situation for you.

Saying "no" is hard if you're not used to saying it. But once you start setting boundaries and letting other people know what those boundaries are, then over time, it gets easier and easier to say "no." If they 'trespass' your limits, then you are well within your rights to tell them off. They might not like it, but they will understand. If they don't, ask them how they'd appreciate it if *you* stepped on *their* boundaries!

Put Yourself Above Others

It's normal to feel guilty when you disappoint other people. But you have to be firm when rejecting someone. If they sense a weakening of resolve, they'll ask you again and again until you give in. If you allow yourself to give in to their pestering, then you'll disappoint *yourself*. You're essentially *transferring* the disappointment from them to you. And you don't want to do that because it's not healthy.

It's unhealthy to say "yes" when you're dying to tell "no" inside.

It's never a good idea to agree to something that goes against your beliefs and principles. When you're not committed to doing something wholeheartedly, your performance is going to suffer. You're not going to deliver what's expected. You'll just end up disappointing yourself and the person who made you say "yes" against your will.

If you have boundaries in place, then you'll be putting your needs and yourself ahead of everyone else. Putting yourself above others is an essential aspect of self-discipline. If you value yourself and your time, then you have to learn how to say "no." You have to accept that you can't please everybody, and you have to believe that you're not the wrong person just because you rejected someone.

In the process of building self-discipline and reaching for your goals, you will need to say no far often than you may like. There's no way around this fact, so the earlier you come to terms with rejecting people, the faster you will grow and the more disciplined you will be.

Just remember that rejection doesn't have to be harsh and rude. Refusal delivered in a kind and gentle manner may result in much better relationships with the people you've rejected.

Chapter 8:

Your Fears and How You Self-Sabotage Your Self-Discipline Efforts

Your success in disciplining yourself starts with you. It doesn't start with your partner, your parents, your friends, or even your therapist. Other people can give you advice and steer you in the right direction, but if you don't do anything, if you fail to take action, then nothing's going to happen.

Taking the first step to achieve self-discipline is always the hardest. During the first few days, you'll probably find yourself resisting your efforts. Other people around you may not be supportive and may downright ridicule you. But once you learn how to block out the noise and do what you need to do, then you're going to find it easier to control yourself, and you'll find yourself growing and moving in the right direction.

Recognizing your fears and your weaknesses is essential to help you set boundaries. This chapter will discuss some of the common concerns and weaknesses that plague people who find it hard to discipline themselves.

Conquering Your Fear Of Failure

Some people find it hard to accept failure. When you grow up in an environment where perfectionism is a must and failure is unacceptable, you naturally grow up afraid of failure.

When you've experienced the adverse effects of previous failures, you acquire the fear of failing again.

You get butterflies in your stomach every time you think about disappointing the people you love. You'd hate for them to be humiliated because of your failure, so you try to avoid doing anything that can cause you, and them, to lose face in front of other people.

A favorite excuse of people who fear failure is the saying "*better safe than sorry*." When you have an irrational fear of failing, you don't give yourself the chance to succeed. You'd rather stay "safe" in your comfort zone. You don't challenge yourself. You're too afraid to try anything new. Or if you do try, you quit far too early because you doubted yourself and didn't think you'd ever succeed. Having this mindset is a huge barrier to your success.

Self-growth is at the bottom of your priorities.

Risks are inherent when taking on new challenges. When you don't take risks, you avoid falling. But intelligent and well-disciplined people know that *not all* risk is bad. Risk can be mitigated by studying and calculating the odds of success.

When setting yourself up to reach a new goal, you try to learn all the details about what you hope to do so you know if your goal is feasible and achievable. If you go back to Chapter 1 and apply the methods I've taught about choosing, specifying, and visualizing your goal, then you're essentially giving yourself no other choice but to succeed.

Being meticulous with your goal planning is essential to minimize risk and failure. If you visualize the process, I showed you in the first chapter, and you should overcome your fear of failure. You will know the exact steps you need to take to realize your goal, and you're essentially leaving very little to chance.

Overcoming Your Fear Of Success

Most people can easily understand or relate to fearing failure.

Fearing success is another matter altogether and is less easily understood by many because its symptoms can easily be mistaken for insecurity and procrastination. In this section, I'll go through the main symptoms that characterize this kind of fear.

The first sign is you feel like *you don't deserve success* or *you feel unworthy.* You're stifling your growth and even greater success because you feel like a charlatan, a fraud. You think someone else deserves your success more than you do because you've been blessed with resources that other people have to work hard to get. You think this gives you an unfair head start, and as such, you don't deserve success.

The second sign of fear of success is when *you fear other people's expectations of you.* You're afraid they'll expect something from you that you can't possibly deliver. Being successful and being in the spotlight can bring about people who expect you to be a constant achiever.

For example, you're afraid that if you become a successful writer, people will expect you to write bestselling novels all the time with captivating storylines and intricate plot twists. You're afraid that people will hate you and stop reading your books if you publish a less than a stellar novel. So because of your fear, you continue writing your fantastic stories on your computer, with no plans of ever publishing them and sharing them with the world.

The third sign is *you're afraid of being isolated.* You don't want people to create a wide berth around you and put you on a pedestal because you're not that kind of person. You still want to hang out with your friends even after you're successful, but you're afraid they're going to keep you at arm's reach, and you don't want that.

You might also have friends who might be jealous of your success and don't want to have anything to do with you anymore simply because they're insecure about *their* lack of success.

The fourth sign is *you're afraid of turning into someone you don't like.* You see it all the time on television. The newly rich and famous suddenly going 180 degrees from their previous lifestyles.

They ditch their husbands, wives, kids, and old friends to chase hot models and party on yachts in the Mediterranean.

You're afraid of turning into a big snob who thinks he can buy everything and everyone with money. You don't want to be one of them, so you don't pursue your dreams and instead continue hiding in your shell.

Lastly, you might be afraid of change; *you might be fearful of the unknown* that success will inevitably bring. You don't want to upset your routines and your current setup at home. You read bedtime stories to your kids now. If you're successful, you'll be so busy with work and managing people and clients that you won't have time for your family, and they'll end up hating you for it.

If you want to pursue success in life, you're going to need self-discipline and self-control to keep on going after what you want. You're going to have to fight against your fear of success because if you don't, then you're not going to get very far in life.

Stop Sabotaging Yourself

The first step to curing your self-sabotaging tendencies is to *acknowledge* that you have a problem. You have to recognize that you have a genuine fear of failure and success because if you don't own up to it, you're not going to find the cure for your 'condition.'

If you think hiding behind a *smiling mask* will hide your fears, you're wrong. You can attain short-term success behind a show, but doing so will take enormous amounts of energy and will eventually sap you of strength. Being true to yourself and acknowledging you have issues is the only way you can stop sabotaging yourself.

Also, try being an *optimist*. When your fears and self-doubt start weighing you down, look beyond the negativity and try to look at the other, the more positive side of things. When you get to thinking there's no way you can succeed, snap yourself out of it because you know that is not true. Many people have successfully overcome the odds stacked against them and have gone on to live fulfilling lives.

Know that you can overcome your fears and find success in almost anything you put your mind to with self-discipline and self-control.

Success doesn't happen overnight. You have to put in the time and the work - to succeed in anything in life. Stop sabotaging your efforts at disciplining yourself!

Chapter 9:

Stay Committed to Your Goals

The road to achieving your long-term goals and objectives is not going to be easy. At first, you may be highly motivated and looking forward to the challenges you may face. However, as time passes by, you slowly start losing that bubbly enthusiasm for reaching your goals. You start allowing yourself to get distracted. You begin missing deadlines you've set for yourself. You start procrastinating and getting lazy. And finally, you decide to jump ship and abandon your quest for success, thus making all your earlier efforts go to waste.

The Power Of Perseverance

In the face of numerous obstacles, challenges, and temptations that we face daily, we sometimes get overwhelmed by it all. Sometimes it's just easier to say "yes" than to communicate "no." But remember that when we say "yes" to temptations and distractions, we say "no" to our goals. And if we say "no" to our goals far too often than is acceptable, then we're ultimately failing ourselves.

Saying "no" is one of the most *powerful* words you can utter if you genuinely want to persevere and succeed. Saying "no" basically means you won't allow yourself to get distracted or get tempted from reaching your goals.

Standing firm and holding your ground is an essential aspect of perseverance. Being stubborn can sometimes be a good thing.

When it comes to going after your goals, the more stubborn and unrelenting you are, the better your chances of success. When you put your head down and start working on your goals, you block out all the noise and the shiny objects that may distract you.

Having grit means being tenacious. It means being focused 100% on your goal. You have your eyes set ahead into the future, and *you ignore the noise* that's doing its best to detract you from your goals. When you have your sights set on the prize, everything else falls into the background. Your self-discipline will guard your thoughts and won't allow you to fall off the wagon and give in to temptation.

If you have the right mindset, that is, if you've already imprinted on your mind that you MUST achieve your goal at any cost, then over time, doing all the tasks you need to do to achieve your goal becomes second nature to you. This is the kind of perseverance and self-discipline that will ultimately lead you to success.

Self-discipline acts as the bridge between your goals and accomplishments. When perseverance and self-control are further factored into this equation, you have the *perfect* recipe for success.

Staying Committed To Your Goal

To succeed in life, you must first have a *solid plan* in place. In Chapter 1 of this book, I shared how important it is that you *visualize your goal and visualize the process* of achieving your goal.

103

Having a constant visible reminder of your goal is a potent motivator. With such a solid plan in place, it's much easier to stay committed to your destination.

Now, if you decide to just "wing" your goal and go with the flow, or whatever you think the quickest way to reaching your goals is, then you're leaving your fate to *luck*.

The word 'commitment' carries a lot of weight and shouldn't be taken lightly. If you're serious about staying committed to your goal, you will have to *put a plan in place* because winging it just won't work. Most importantly, if you have self-discipline, you will not leave your success to 'luck.' Being disciplined will keep you straight and narrow and help you stay committed to your goal.

Breaking down your goals into *mini-goals* is also essential as it makes a herculean task seem so much easier. For example, if you're thinking of buying up a $250,000 house within 2 years, then you can try to break down the amount you must save.

It's much easier to say you'll save $10,500 per month for 24 months than just saying you'll ' *have that amount a week or so before your intended purchase date.*' What if you don't raise that amount? What will happen to your goal? Based on this example, you can easily see that breaking down the amount you need to save per month is the right step in committing to the goal.

It's also important to note the distinction between being *committed* and just being *interested*. Commitment means you're willing to see something through to the end.

In terms of reaching your goals, it means doing whatever it takes to reach your goals.

Interest, on the other hand, is just being intrigued by the thought of possibly achieving something. It's like window shopping.

You're just looking through the glass and appreciating what you see inside, but you're not willing to commit and spend money on any of the stuff they're selling inside.

If you genuinely want to succeed with your goals, then you're going to have to be more than interested. You're going to have to be a hundred percent committed, and you're going to do all it takes to succeed.

Chapter 10:

Rewarding Self-Discipline

As humans, we all love getting rewarded for our good deeds. And one of the essential aspects of self-discipline that you shouldn't neglect is *rewarding yourself.* Self-rewards help reinforce the habits and routines we've established so we can reach our goals faster.

If you don't practice rewarding yourself, you'll soon find yourself losing motivation, and you may start giving a lackluster performance. You'll start feeling sluggish. Doing your tasks would be a chore, a heavy burden, whereas you could do the same jobs in less than half the time when you started.

Rewarding yourself with something you want is very important because it's what you associate doing your tasks with. You can promise yourself that if you do a good job and finish your chores before lunch, then you can treat yourself to that fancy new restaurant later tonight. There are many possibilities of things you can reward yourself with, and it's essential to know a few guidelines to make sure your rewards don't cause you to lose sight of your main goal.

A Fitting Reward

Rewards can come in many different shapes and sizes, and you know best the kind of rewards you'd like to give yourself.

For best results, you should develop a reward system that will motivate you immediately, in the medium term, and for a long time.

It can be something small like a quick trip to the grocery store or maybe an hour's worth of surfing on Facebook for immediate rewards.

Perhaps even a bit of that chocolate cake that's been sitting in your fridge for two weeks now (just don't do this too often).

It can be something you do for medium-term rewards when you accomplish a monthly goal, such as buying a new shirt or a new dress. In the long-term, you may wish to reward yourself with a weekend staycation at your favorite hotel in your famous city or maybe even take an entire week off and travel to take your mind off your daily grind.

Another excellent reward you can give yourself is to do charitable activities by volunteering at a shelter or donating to charity. You don't have to give away money. Instead, you can give a bit of your time to lend a helping hand to people in need.

Helping other people can give you a tremendous sense of self-accomplishment and is suitable for your self-esteem and personal growth.

Not all rewards are created equally, though. Don't choose a prize that's going to be *counterproductive* to your goals.

Remember the reason why you're rewarding yourself – it's for a job well done. You don't want to undo anything you've done so that you can say you've given yourself a nice reward.

Let me give you a scenario here. For instance, your long-term goal is to save $100,000 by year-end. To meet your goal, you would need to save up at least $8,400 every single month for the next 12 months.

You can choose to reward yourself every month every time you deposit $8,400 into your bank account. It can be something like buying yourself a new pair of shoes (nothing too expensive) or maybe having dinner with your family at a nice restaurant.

What you shouldn't do is splurge and spend hundreds or even thousands of dollars on something you're going to end up regretting anyway. If you can afford to pay that kind of money on a 'reward,' maybe you should try investing it so you can at least see some ROI (return on investment). With this kind of mindset, you'll have your $100K by the end of the year, plus you'll have some money coming in from the investments you've rewarded yourself with!

An alternative situation will be if your long-term goal is to lose 25% of your body weight within 10 months. It would help if you weren't rewarding yourself by going to buffets and all-you-can-eat restaurants because you'll essentially be undoing all the hard work you've done on your body.

When you think about it, you're not rewarding yourself as you're punishing your body with food when you've worked hard to lose all that extra weight. A good reward, for example, might be buying some new exercise equipment that's easier on your joints and takes up little space in your house.

Eventually, you'll end up with a mini-gym in your house or your office, and you'll no longer need to pay for a gym membership (unless, of course, you crave company, then going to the gym would be better for you to help motivate you).

The key takeaway here is that you have to *choose a reward that's aligned with your goals.* Never reward yourself with something

that will undo your hard work; instead, try to reward yourself with something that will help you reach your goals.

Delaying Gratification

Not many people will have the discipline to delay gratification.

In fact, with the leaps and bounds in modern technology, we can have almost everything we want at practically the push of a button. And this is where you, with your self-discipline, will stand out from the crowd. If you're disciplined, it will be easier for you to say "no" to instant gratification and wait for some time before rewarding yourself.

In seeking immediate rewards, you can instead pat yourself on the back and praise yourself. Then you can encourage yourself to wait just a little bit more and do some more work before you finally reward yourself with a nice treat. This practice is self-discipline at its finest.

Acknowledging your self-discipline provides a *significant mental boost* and allows you to *build your self-confidence*, too.

Encouraging yourself to continue doing what you're doing does amazing wonders for yourself. And don't think only the crazies talk to themselves because we ALL speak to ourselves. You need to block out all the nonsense and negative thoughts in your head and focus only on cheerful mental chatter.

Another essential benefit of delaying gratification is you're *strengthening your self-control*, too. If you've set your mind to only rewarding yourself after you've done a particular task, then you will do your best to make sure you finish the assignment early and to a good standard (nope, haphazard quality work doesn't count).

Otherwise, if you fail to complete it, then you will not be rewarding yourself.

For instance, if you're planning to reward yourself with a movie ticket to the newest Hollywood blockbuster, then you'll stop procrastinating and Googling details about the movie and its leading stars, where it was filmed, and maybe even some funny bloopers.

Instead, you'll close out unnecessary tabs on your browser and laser-focus on your tasks.

You'll also tell yourself that if you don't finish within the day, then you can kiss that movie ticket goodbye because you won't be watching it on the big screen.

With any luck, it might be on Netflix in a few months, but you know just how awesome it feels when you're watching a movie in a darkened theatre with a hundred other people screaming and laughing with you!

Delaying gratification is an excellen*t exercise for improving your focus and concentration*. It keeps procrastination at bay and motivates you to do more so you can reward yourself. In some ways, it is like stressing yourself in tiny doses, but this is not the wrong kind of stress, mind you. It's eustress or good pressure, just like what you learned in Chapter 6. Managing good stress is relatively easy if you have self-discipline, and when coupled with a sound rewards system, you can reach your goals with small steps in the right direction.

Conclusion

Disciplining yourself can be a long, lonely journey. But the rewards you'll reap with being punished are virtually limitless.

Whatever you set your mind to do and achieve, whether it's a short-term or long-term goal, is very much possible if you have the discipline to do what's necessary to complete your plan. You can be anything you want to be.

Start your journey by knowing your why and why you need self-discipline in your life. Then you need to visualize your goals and the processes you need to carry out to reach your goal.

You have to have a roadmap to success, so you need to be as specific as possible and leave very little to chance.

Building good, habit-forming routines that will help you achieve your goals is necessary. I've detailed how having a morning ritual habit is essential for your self-discipline. Also, since stress is inevitable, you'll have to learn how to manage and control pressure, so it doesn't affect your goals.

Keeping yourself fit and healthy is essential to manage stress.

I am eating healthy, exercising regularly, and getting a good night's sleep, all to play a significant role in getting stress down to a manageable level.

To succeed at disciplining yourself, you'll need to learn how to set boundaries and say no to temptations and distractions. You'll also need to stop sabotaging yourself and learn how to overcome your fears and insecurities because if you don't, you'll never leave your comfort zone and never get anywhere in life.

Rewarding yourself also plays a vital role in disciplining yourself, mainly if you apply delayed gratification. You can keep your mind focused on getting a reward for a job well done, and you'll do your best to make sure you get that reward.

Self-discipline is one of the greatest equalizers known to man. You may start at the bottom rung of your organization, but you'll make it to the top sooner or later with hard work and discipline.

You may not have been lucky enough to have anything handed to you on a silver platter but with your determination and self-discipline,

you'll soon surpass those who had a big head start.

If you apply all the strategies I've written in this book, you'll be a self-discipline master in no time at all. With self-discipline, you'll have the mental strength to stop making excuses, you'll be able to resist any temptation that comes your way, and you'll find it easier to reach your goals in life finally.